EMMA FORBES'
GOING LIVE!
COOKBOOK

BBC BOOKS

SAFETY HINTS

1 Ask permission before you start cooking and if in doubt over anything, always ask the advice of the nearest available adult!

2 Wash your hands before starting to cook, and try to remember to clear up afterwards. If you leave a messy kitchen you may not be allowed to cook again!

3 Never put anything in or take anything out of the oven without using oven gloves.

4 When cooking with oil, be very careful – *never* bend over it and don't get too close. Don't drop anything into hot oil or water – it will splash – and never lean across hot pans – steam is dangerous.

5 Take great care whenever chopping or slicing anything – keep your fingers clear of the knife. Take care, too, when using graters or peelers.

6 Remember that saucepan handles can get very hot whilst in use. Turn them to the side when cooking so you don't knock into them.

7 When cooking on a hob, don't put anything too near that could melt or burn.

8 When using an electric mixer with sharp blades or attachments, always make sure you keep your hands well clear while it's switched on, and *never* touch a plug with wet hands.

9 If you have a younger brother, sister or friend helping, remember to watch over them and don't let them use anything sharp or touch anything hot.

10 Leave things that need to cool somewhere where they won't be touched. Remember to turn off the oven when you have finished.

11 Watch out for this symbol ⚡ throughout the book as it is there to warn you of anything dangerous.

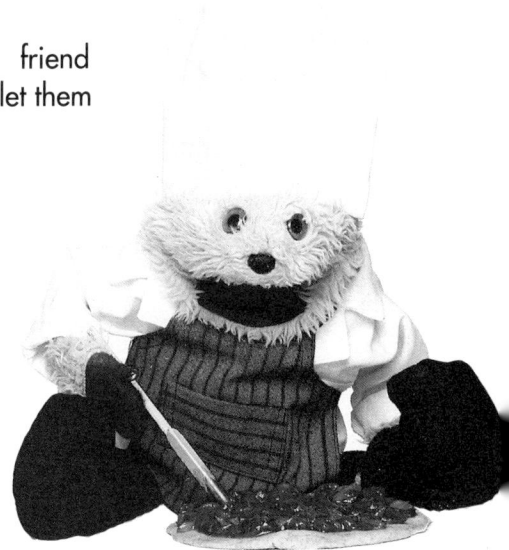

EMMA FORBES' GOING LIVE! COOKBOOK

For my 'Chief Taster', Graham
and
for Chris, for making it all possible

FOREWORD

If you've watched Phillip, Gordon and me cooking on *Going Live!*, you will have seen just how much fun it can be! Although things often go wrong, the end result is always delicious, and as you've also probably noticed, we can demonstrate how to turn a disaster into a success!

As long as you realise that it doesn't matter if things don't look totally perfect and that cooking really isn't that difficult, you'll be amazed at what you can make – and once you get the hang of it, you can experiment with different ingredients and create your own recipes.

This book not only contains some of the tried and tested recipes from past series of *Going Live!*, but also lots of new and exciting dishes which are easy to prepare, healthy, delicious, and guarantee stunning results that will convince you to get into that kitchen and *get cooking!*

ACKNOWLEDGEMENTS

I would like to thank everyone who has helped put
this book together with me, and I would also like to
give a huge thank you to the whole of the *Going
Live!* team for all their support and help and for
always eating everything I cook! Finally, a thank
you to my great cooking partner, Phillip.

Published by BBC Books,
a division of BBC Enterprises Limited,
Woodlands, 80 Wood Lane, London W12 0TT

First published 1992
© Emma Forbes 1992
Gordon the gopher,
© Gordon the gopher Trading Company 1987

ISBN 0 563 36409 2

Designed by Sara Kidd

Photographs by Simon Fowler and Chris Turner
Styling by Cathy Sinker
Home Economists Rebecca Money and Ricky Turner
Make-up by Mary Ellen Lamb for Michaeljohn
Set in Futura by Goodfellow & Egan Ltd
Printed and bound in Great Britain by Clays Ltd, St Ives plc
Colour separations by Dot Gradations, Chelmsford
Cover printed by Clays Ltd, St Ives plc

CONTENTS

PHIL'S PANCAKES

Why do we only eat pancakes on Pancake Day? They make a fantastic Sunday breakfast – sweet or savoury – and they can be a real laugh to make, particularly the 'tossing' out of the pan!

STEP **1** Put the flour and salt into a large mixing bowl and make a well in the middle. Crack the egg into the well.

STEP **2** Gradually pour in the milk, whisking constantly to avoid any lumps, until the mixture is well blended. ▶

100 g (4 oz) plain flour
A pinch of salt
1 egg
300 ml (10 fl oz) milk
Butter or oil for frying

1

2

STEP **3** ⚡ Pour about ½ tablespoon of oil, or put a little knob of butter, into a frying pan or skillet and turn the hob on to quite a high heat. Take a large serving spoon of the mixture, pour it into the pan and quickly swish it around to cover the base.

STEP **5** ⚡ Once flipped, cook for the same amount of time on the other side – you should be able to see when it's done – and serve immediately with any filling of your choice.

' ***I don't have any tips for stopping a pancake from landing on the floor – other than to pick it up, throw it away and start again!*** '

S T E P

4

Leave the pancake cooking until bubbles start appearing on the surface.

✐ Push around the edge with a wooden spoon, to loosen the pancake, and shake it a little. It is now ready to toss on to the other side – if you dare!

IDEAS FOR FILLINGS

Sliced banana and maple syrup

Chopped grilled bacon and cream cheese

Cheese and pickle

Fruit salad and Greek yoghurt

Ice-cream and chocolate sauce

Honey and lemon

Chopped apple, cinnamon and raisins

Sliced tomato, chopped basil and grated mozzarella cheese

The list is endless!

OUTRAGEOUS OATMEAL COOKIES

Friends coming round and nothing to snack on? These are the perfect solution because they contain ingredients that you can virtually guarantee to have hanging around the house and they can be whipped up in a flash.

STEP 1 ⚡ Pre-heat the oven to gas mark 4, 180°C (350°F). Lightly grease 2 baking sheets. Mix the flour, oats, cinnamon and baking powder together in a bowl.

STEP 2 In another bowl, beat together the butter and sugars until light and creamy. Then add the egg, vanilla essence, golden syrup and finally the flour mixture, making sure it is well blended. ▶

75 g (3 oz) self-raising flour
100 g (4 oz) porridge oats
½ teaspoon cinnamon
½ teaspoon baking powder
100 g (4 oz) butter
75 g (3 oz) brown sugar
75 g (3 oz) caster sugar
1 egg
½ teaspoon vanilla essence
2 tablespoons golden syrup

1

2

STEP 3

Take 1 heaped teaspoon at a time and press flat on to the baking sheet until all the mixture is used.

🗲 Bake in the oven for 10 to 12 minutes, or until they turn golden brown. Leave to cool on a wire rack – they get crispier as they get colder.

Here's another recipe using oats and similar ingredients . . .

MELT-IN-YOUR-MOUTH CRUMBLE

SERVES 4

For the inside:
25 g (1 oz) butter
4 apples, peeled, cored and chopped
2 tablespoons brown sugar
2 bananas, peeled and chopped
300 ml (10 fl oz) orange juice

For the crumble:
100 g (4 oz) porridge oats
50 g (2 oz) plain wholemeal flour
1 tablespoon golden syrup
50 g (2 oz) brown sugar
1/2 teaspoon cinnamon
2 tablespoons desiccated coconut
2 tablespoons any chopped nuts or nuts and raisins
100 g (4 oz) butter, softened

Pre-heat the oven to gas mark 5, 190°C (375°F).

In a small saucepan melt the butter, add the apples and sugar and stir over the heat until the apples soften and the sugar disappears.

Place the bananas in a shallow ovenproof dish. Pour in the orange juice, add the apples and spread them out.

In a bowl, mix all the crumble ingredients until they have stuck together and resemble large breadcrumbs. Sprinkle over the fruit until it's covered.

Bake for 15 to 20 minutes until golden and bubbling. Serve immediately.

GORDON'S GREAT GOULASH

One of Gordon's best dishes, this is perfect for a cold winter's evening. It's also very filling, especially if served either with a baked potato or on a bed of boiled or steamed rice.

STEP 1

✒ Pre-heat the oven to gas mark 3, 160°C (325°F).

In a flameproof casserole dish, heat the butter and oil. Mix the paprika with the flour and roll the stewing steak in it until it is completely covered. Then gently fry it until browned.

STEP 2

✒ Add the onion and carrots, and stir over the heat for a couple of minutes. ▶

> '*The longer you cook a goulash on a low heat in the oven, the more tender the meat is and the better the sauce.*'

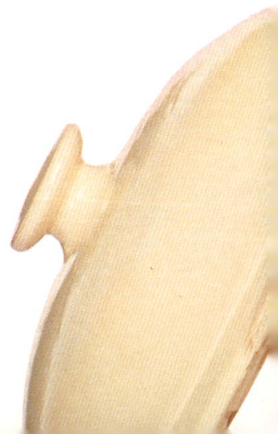

25 g (1 oz) butter
1 dessertspoon sunflower oil
2 teaspoons paprika
1 tablespoon plain flour
450 g (1 lb) lean stewing
  steak, cut into chunks
1 onion, peeled and chopped
4 carrots, peeled and
  chopped
2 beef stock cubes dissolved
  in 450 ml (15 fl oz) hot
  water
2 tablespoons tomato purée
2 bay leaves
salt and freshly ground
  black pepper, to taste
1 × 400 g (14 oz) tin
  cannellini beans, drained
2 tablespoons natural
  yoghurt

1

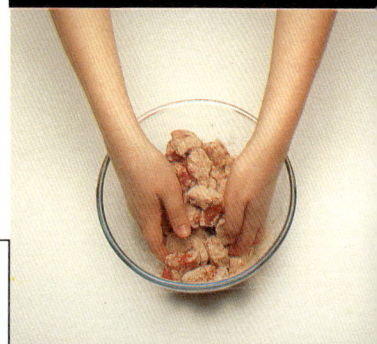

2

15

STEP **3**

⚡ Pour in the stock, and add the tomato purée, bay leaves, salt and pepper, and the beans. Give a good stir, put on the lid and cook in the oven for 2½ to 3 hours. Check on it occasionally and give it a stir.

MIGHTY HERBY MUFFINS

MAKES 12 TO 15 MUFFINS

200 g (7 oz) plain or wholemeal self-raising flour

2 teaspoons baking powder

1 teaspoon salt

1 tablespoon poppy seeds

2 teaspoons dried thyme (or any other herb)

2 eggs

100 ml (3 1/2 fl oz) milk

50 ml (2 fl oz) sunflower or vegetable oil

40 g (1 1/2 oz) Parmesan cheese, grated (or any other hard cheese such as Cheddar or Edam)

S T E P **4**

Serve from the casserole with a spoonful of natural yoghurt on the top.

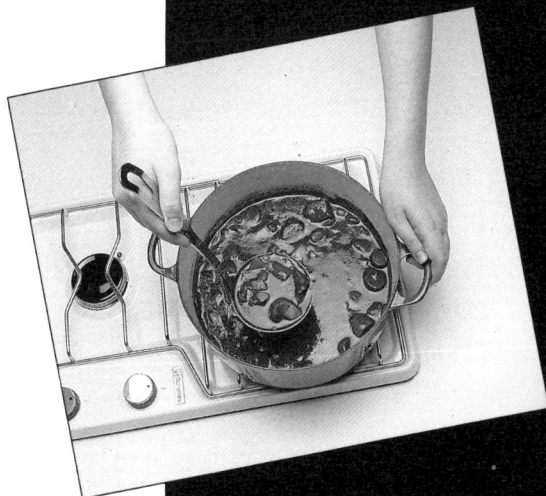

✏ Pre-heat the oven to gas mark 6, 200°C (400°F). Grease some muffin tins.

Mix together all the dry ingredients in a bowl: the flour, baking powder, salt, poppy seeds and herbs.

Beat 2 eggs, then add them to the bowl with the milk, oil and cheese, and mix well until a smooth batter is formed.

Spoon a little mixture into each bun tin.

✏ Bake them in the oven for 15 to 20 minutes, or until risen and golden. Transfer to a wire rack to cool slightly, then serve warm.

' Serve the muffins warm in a basket, or alternatively split them or make a cross on the top and spread with some home-made herb and garlic butter. Mix about 50g (2 oz) of softened butter with 2 teaspoons of any chopped fresh herbs and 1 clove of finely chopped garlic ... yum! '

'ROMANCE-IN-THE-AIR' VALENTINE CAKE

Make Valentine's Day a special day – make a heart-shaped cake for your nearest and dearest, whoever that might be. . .

STEP **1** Pre-heat the oven to gas mark 6, 200°C (400°F). Take a piece of greaseproof paper and draw round a 20 cm (8 in) heart-shaped cake tin. Cut out the shape, place in the bottom of the tin and grease the whole of the inside thoroughly. Mix together the flour, cocoa powder and baking powder in a bowl.

STEP **2** In another bowl, beat together the eggs, sugar and vanilla essence until light and fluffy. Then beat in the mayonnaise. ▶

225 g (8 oz) plain flour
50 g (2 oz) cocoa powder
2 teaspoons baking powder
3 eggs
225 g (8 oz) caster sugar
1 teaspoon vanilla essence
175 g (6 oz) mayonnaise
50 ml (2 fl oz) milk
225 g (8 oz) chocolate,
    melted

1

2

S T E P 3

Add the flour and then the milk to the egg mixture, bit by bit. Add the melted chocolate and continue to mix until completely blended.

CHOCOLATE FUDGE ICING

75 g (3 oz) butter, softened
1–2 teaspoons warm water
150 g (5 oz) icing sugar
1/4 teaspoon vanilla essence
25 g (1 oz) cocoa or chocolate
  powder

Mix everything together in a large bowl. If the consistency is not quite right, add a little more water until it seems spreadable.

'*They say that the way to a man's heart is through his stomach . . . that's definitely true of Gordon!*'

4

⚡ Pour the mixture into the cake tin and bake for 25 to 30 minutes, or until a knife inserted in the centre comes out clean. Leave to cool on a wire rack before removing from the tin. Then decorate . . .

' **Serve a small slice with some sliced strawberries and whipped cream . . .** '

WRAP-UP CHICKEN

This is a simple-to-make, but impressive, dish that could be served at a party – and by wrapping it in kitchen foil the chicken becomes slightly more unusual.

STEP 1

⚡ Pre-heat the oven to gas mark 5, 190°C (375°F).
In a large bowl, whisk together all the ingredients (except the chicken breasts and lemon slices) with a fork until really well blended. Then leave on one side. ▶

'*If you're planning on kissing anyone, it might be a good idea to leave out the garlic!*'

1 clove garlic, peeled and
   finely chopped
1 teaspoon fresh tarragon or
   sage, finely chopped (or
   ½ teaspoon dried)
2 tablespoons runny honey
1½ tablespoons Dijon
   mustard
2 tablespoons sunflower or
   olive oil
Juice of 1 lemon
1 tablespoon soy sauce
Salt and freshly ground
   black pepper, to taste.
4 boned, skinned chicken
   breasts
4 slices lemon
(4 × 20cm (8 in) squares
   kitchen foil)

1

STEP 2

Fold each sheet of kitchen foil in half, and then place one chicken breast in the centre of each sheet. Scrunch up the ends of each sheet to make a boat shape with an opening along the top.

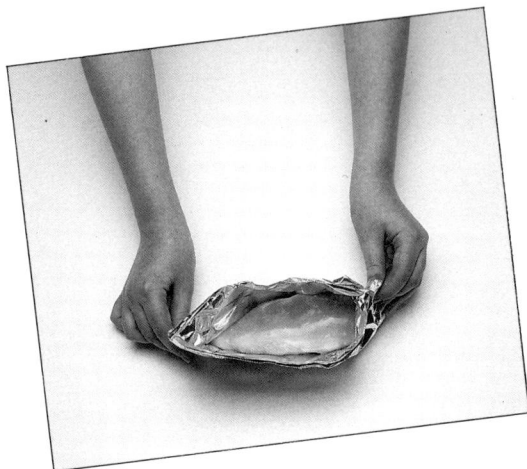

If you're not a great meat-eater, or even if you are, try this yummy vegetable bake . . .

A VEGGIE FEAST

SERVES 4

40 g (1½ oz) butter
1 small onion, finely chopped
2 tablespoons wholemeal flour
120 ml (4 fl oz) milk
2 eggs, beaten
Salt and freshly ground
    pepper, to taste
50 g (2 oz) cheese, grated
1 tablespoon tomato sauce
1 tablespoon mixed herbs

2 teaspoons English mustard
275 g (10 oz) cooked brown
    or white long-grain rice
3 sticks celery, finely chopped
1 small can sweetcorn,
    drained
½ red or green pepper, finely
    chopped
2 leeks, finely chopped

STEP 3

Pour the sauce over the chicken breasts, top with a slice of lemon and then seal up the parcels. ✦ Bake in the oven for about 40 minutes.

Carefully open one parcel to check the chicken is thoroughly cooked – the juices will run clear, not red, if you push in a skewer. Then serve the parcels for your guests to open themselves.

• •

✦ Pre-heat the oven to gas mark 6, 200°C (400°F). Grease a 23 cm (9 in) cake tin. In a small saucepan, melt the butter, add the onion and fry until soft. Add the flour, stir for a minute, then add the milk and stir until the sauce thickens. In another bowl, beat together the eggs and salt and pepper to taste. Add the cheese, tomato sauce, herbs, mustard and rice and stir. Add the sauce, and finally stir in all the chopped vegetables before pouring into the cake tin.

✦ Bake for 20 to 30 minutes until set. Turn out, slice and serve hot or cold. Use any vegetables you like for this recipe.

‘ *Wrap-Up Chicken is delicious served with a hot steamed salad. Take a mixture of any of your favourite vegetables, cut them into pieces and lightly steam them for 5 minutes. Drizzle some Simple Salad Dressing (page 38) over the top and eat while hot.* ’

25

FRUIT SALAD ON A STICK

This makes the average fruit salad seem dull by comparison. It's great for having at parties or to keep in the fridge for a low-cal snack.

STEP 1
Simply thread the fruit on to the skewers, alternating the fresh with the dried, and arrange on a plate.

STEP 2
Mix together the dressing ingredients and pour it over the top. Eat with your fingers!

FORBES FUNKY FISH CAKES

This is a really fun way to eat fish – you just need to make sure that you watch out for any bones floating around. As shops often order for the weekend, fish is at its freshest on a Friday, so make this something for that Friday feeling.

STEP 1
⚡ Pre-heat the oven to gas mark 4, 180°C (350°F).
Place the fish in a shallow ovenproof dish and just cover with milk. Bake in the oven for 15 to 20 minutes until cooked. Leave to cool. ▶

1

MAKES 2 SKEWERS PER PERSON

Any chunks of fruit –
   pineapples, apples, kiwi
   fruits, bananas,
   strawberries, dates
Any dried fruit – apricots,
   prunes, figs, pears,
   apples, (soaked
   overnight)
Long wooden sticks or
   skewers

For the poppy seed dressing:
2 teaspoons poppy seeds
2 teaspoons runny honey
1 tablespoon lemon juice

MAKES ABOUT 8

275 g (10 oz) salmon, cod or
   any white fish
150 ml (5 fl oz) milk
½ teaspoon salt
¼ teaspoon black pepper
450 g (1 lb) boiled potatoes
   mashed with 2
   tablespoons milk and 1
   tablespoon butter
1 egg
2 slices brown bread, made
   into breadcrumbs
1 heaped tablespoon
   wholemeal flour
50 g (2 oz) spinach leaves,
   finely chopped
4 spring onions, finely
   chopped
1 teaspoon chopped fresh
   parsley
2 tablespoons sunflower oil

27

STEP **2** Flake the fish and remove any bones. Put it in a bowl with some salt and pepper, the mashed potato, egg, breadcrumbs, flour, spinach, spring onions and parsley. Stir until combined together. Make handfuls into balls and pat into flat shapes.

' ***This tastes good served on a bed of Home-made Tomato Sauce (page 36).*** '

EXPERT

3

⚡ Heat the oil in a frying pan and add the fish cakes, a couple at a time. Cook until browned on both sides. Turn them a couple more times to make sure they cook all the way through.

Once cooked, drain on some kitchen paper to get rid of any excess oil, and serve immediately.

‘ *Try using different varieties of fish mixed together – cod and salmon, or haddock and cod – or try smoked haddock for an interesting alternative.* ’

SPICED EASTER APPLE BARS

If you have a sweet tooth but are aware of eating too many sweets, try these as an alternative – they are healthy, full of good things and also yummy! The smell always reminds me of Easter, and they're a wonderful change from loads of chocolate Easter eggs!

STEP 1

⚡ Pre-heat the oven to gas mark 6, 200°C (400°F). Grease a 23cm (9in) square cake tin.

In a large bowl, mix together all the dry ingredients: the flour, salt, baking powder, nutmeg and cloves. ▶

100 g (4 oz) plain flour
½ teaspoon salt
1 tablespoon baking powder
1 teaspoon ground nutmeg
¼ teaspoon ground cloves
   or ground ginger
75 g (3 oz) butter
100 g (4 oz) brown sugar
2 eggs
3 eating apples, peeled,
   cored and grated
1 teaspoon vanilla essence
75 g (3 oz) raisins
75 g (3 oz) chopped dates
50 g (2 oz) chopped nuts
   (almonds, walnuts,
   cashews, etc.)

1

STEP **2** ✔ In a small saucepan, melt together the butter and sugar, stirring constantly.

STEP **4** ✔ Spread the mixture evenly into the tin and bake in the oven for 20-25 minutes, or until a knife inserted in the centre comes out clean. Leave to cool a little then cut into 12 bars and transfer to a wire rack to finish cooling.

You could then add some vanilla icing . . .

VANILLA ICING

25 g (1 oz) butter, softened
175 g (6 oz) icing sugar
½ teaspoon vanilla essence
1 tablespoon milk

Mix everything together until well combined.

3

Mix the eggs, grated apples and vanilla essence into the flour, then add the melted butter and sugar. Finally, stir in the raisins, dates and nuts.

' *These are best left overnight in the fridge. Once cooled they become really chewy.* '

EXPERT

PERFECT PIZZAS

The great thing about making your own pizza dough is that you can really tell that it's home–made, and once you've mastered the technique, you can go into business!

STEP **1** ✒ Pre-heat the oven to gas mark 4, 180°C (350°F).

In a large bowl, mix the flour and salt together. Then add the butter and mix them all together until the mixture resembles fine breadcrumbs.

STEP **2** ✒ In a small saucepan, heat the milk and water together until just warm (*not* boiling). Take out a little of the liquid and mix it with the yeast in a cup until it forms a smooth paste, and then add it to the flour along with the rest of the liquid. ▶

450 g (1lb) strong white
    flour or 225 g (8 oz)
    strong plain flour and
    225g (8 oz) strong
    wholemeal flour
1 teaspoon salt
50 g (2 oz) butter, softened
150 ml (5 fl oz) milk
150 ml (5 fl oz) water
25 g (1 oz) fast action dried
    yeast (1 sachet)

1

2

STEP **3** Mix together until a pliable dough is formed using a mixer (or your hands). To begin with it will be very sticky, so just keep adding a little flour. Knead for approximately 5 to 10 minutes.

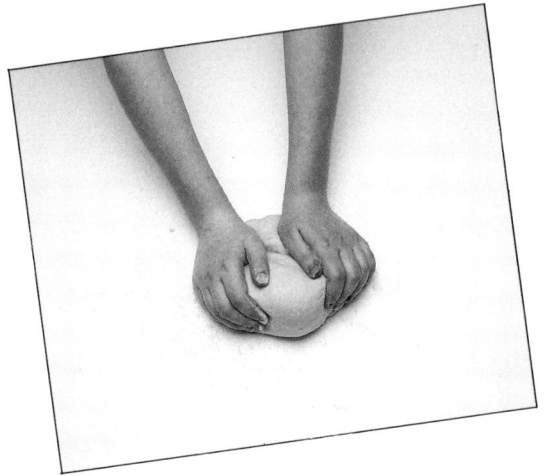

STEP **5** Cut the risen dough into 8 pieces for small pizzas, or 4 pieces for large ones. Roll and pat the dough out to about the size of a dinner plate. Then place the dough on to a large greased baking sheet and leave them to rise again for about another 20 minutes.

THE BEST HOME-MADE TOMATO SAUCE

2 tablespoons sunflower or olive oil

1 small onion, peeled and finely chopped

1 tablespoon cornflour

1 × 400 g (14 oz) tin chopped tomatoes or 10 fresh tomatoes, skinned and chopped

1 tablespoon tomato purée

2 tablespoons dried basil or 6 fresh basil leaves finely chopped

2 teaspoons brown sugar

Salt and freshly ground black pepper

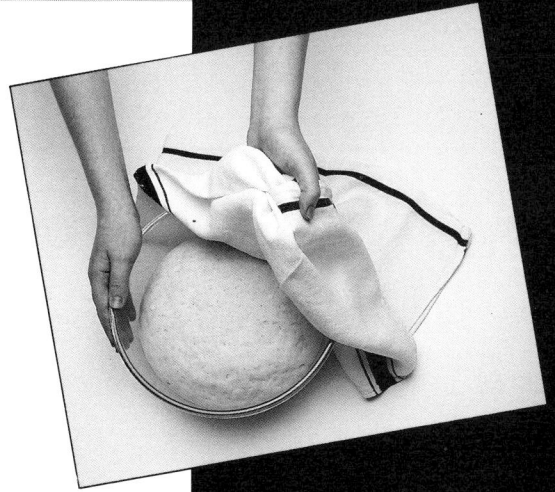

STEP **4**

Cover the dough with a tea towel and leave it to rise in a bowl in a warm place for about half an hour, or until the mixture has doubled in size.

STEP **6**

✎ Finally, spoon some tomato sauce over the top and add any of your favourite toppings before baking for approx 15 to 20 minutes, or until bubbling and golden on top. Serve immediately.

✎ In a saucepan, heat the oil and cook the onion until transparent. Quickly add the cornflour and keep stirring over a low heat, making sure that it doesn't go lumpy. Pour in the tomatoes, tomato purée, basil, brown sugar and salt and pepper to taste. Stir until blended and continue to cook over a low heat until gently bubbling.

' **Why not try this home-made tomato sauce rather than the shop-bought variety!** '

SENSATIONAL SUMMER SALAD

A salad doesn't have to be boring, it can be as exotic and imaginative as you want to make it, and if you add enough extras it can be a meal in itself! This just happens to be one of my favourite combinations.

STEP 1

✦ Simply chop up all the ingredients and assemble them in a pretty design in a salad bowl.

Mix together all the dressing ingredients and drizzle the dressing over the top just before serving.

> **' Don't stick exactly to the ingredients I've given here. The great thing about salads is that you can add whatever you like. '**

SIMPLE SALAD DRESSING

150 ml (5 fl oz) olive or
  sunflower oil
2 teaspoons Dijon mustard
2 tablespoons tarragon
  vinegar
Salt and freshly ground black
  pepper, to taste
1 teaspoon brown sugar or
  honey
Juice of ½ lemon

Mix all the ingredients together until well combined.

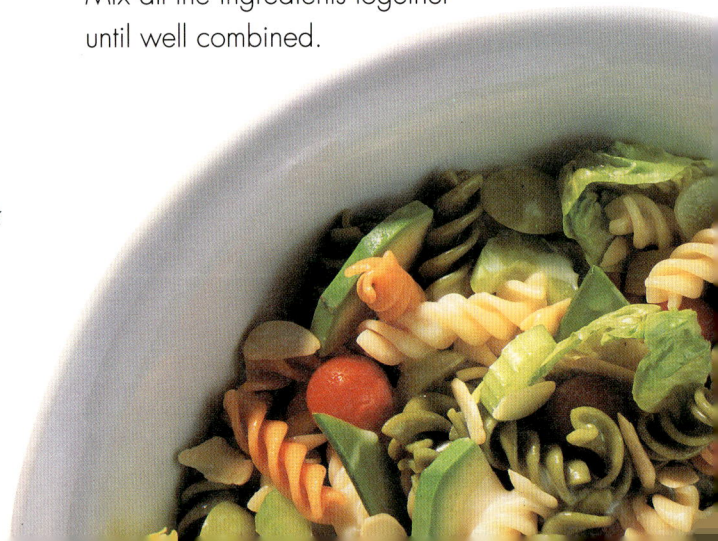

1 eating apple, cored and
  chopped
2 handfuls of cooked pasta
  shapes
2 lettuce hearts, chopped
1/4 cucumber, sliced
A handful of seedless
  grapes, halved
A handful of mange-tout
8 baby tomatoes, whole
2 sticks celery, chopped
25 g (1 oz) flaked almonds
1/2 ripe avocado, peeled and
  chopped

For the lemony dressing:
2 tablespoons olive oil
Juice of 1/2 lemon
2 teaspoons runny honey
5 tablespoons Greek yoghurt

1

CHOCOHOLICS CHOC-CHIP HAZELNUT BROWNIES

These are for the real chocoholics amongst us. Don't eat these every day of the week, but if you're going to go all the way, try them with a scoop of vanilla ice-cream.

STEP 1

✒ Pre-heat the oven to gas mark 4, 180°C (350°F). Grease a 20cm (8in) square cake tin. Place the butter and chocolate in the top of a double boiler. Half fill the bottom with water, bring it to a simmer and gently melt the butter and chocolate over a low heat.

STEP 3

✒ Sprinkle the hazelnuts and chocolate chips over the top of the mixture, which may be hot, and press them down.

75 g (3 oz) butter, softened
50 g (2 oz) plain chocolate
225 g (8 oz) caster sugar
2 eggs, beaten
½ teaspoon vanilla essence
75 g (3 oz) plain flour
50 g (2 oz) hazelnuts, chopped (or any other type of nut)
50 g (2 oz) chocolate chips

STEP 2

Remove from the heat and add to the bowl containing the sugar, eggs and vanilla essence, and stirring quickly, blend well. Fold in the flour and then spoon the mixture into the cake tin.

STEP 4

⚡ Bake in the oven 30 to 35 minutes, or until a knife inserted in the centre comes out clean. Leave to cool in the tin before cutting into squares.

41

MAD MARMALADE ROLL

Serve very small slices of this roll - it's delicious but very rich. The 'rolling' of this can only provide endless laughs – it's almost guaranteed to crack, but it doesn't matter, it looks better slightly imperfect!

STEP 1

⚡ Pre-heat the oven to gas mark 4, 180°C (350°F). Line a 40 × 28 cm (16 × 11 in) jam-roll tin with greased greaseproof paper.

STEP 2

Beat the eggs until pale and thick, then gradually beat in the sugar. Add the water and vanilla essence, then the flour, baking powder, salt and ground almonds, beating until the batter is smooth. ▶

3 eggs
175 g (6 oz) caster sugar
50 ml (2 fl oz) water
1 teaspoon vanilla essence
75 g (3 oz) plain flour
1 teaspoon baking powder
¼ teaspoon salt
25 g (1 oz) ground almonds
Orange or lemon marmalade

Tea whipped cream:
120 ml (4 fl oz) whipping
    cream
3 tablespoons icing sugar
2 tablespoons of strong tea
    from a cup of black tea
½ teaspoon vanilla essence
50 ml (2 fl oz) fromage frais
Icing sugar, to decorate

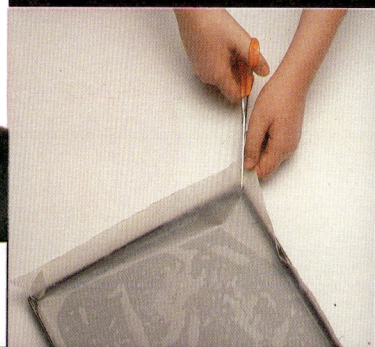

1

2

STEP **3**

⚡ Pour into the tin and bake in the oven for 12 to 15 minutes, or until a toothpick inserted in the centre comes out clean. Loosen the cake from the edges with a blunt knife and turn out on to another sheet of greaseproof paper, and peel off the first sheet. Leave to cool.

STEP **5**

Whip together all the ingredients for the cream and when thick and blended, spread over the top of the marmalade using a spatula (not too thick – if there is some spare, save it!)

STEP **6**

Carefully roll the roll away from you using the greaseproof paper to help, and transfer it on to a plate. Sprinkle with icing sugar, chill in the fridge for at least 1 hour and serve cut into thin slices.

4

Spread the roll generously with marmalade, making sure you cover the whole surface.

EXPERT

' *If you cut two slices and place them side by side on a plate with a thin slice of banana down the middle, it looks like a butterfly!* '

BONFIRE NIGHT PERFECT PASTA BAKE

Everybody loves pasta – it's filling, cheap and you can add almost anything to it. This is one of my favourites, but for a simpler dish just boil some pasta and serve it with some of my Home-Made Tomato Sauce (page 36), freshly grated Parmesan cheese and chopped basil – *yum!*

STEP **1**

Pre-heat the oven to gas mark 4, 180°C (350°F).

Bring a large saucepan of salted water to the boil, add the pasta and stir.

Bring back to the boil, stir again, cover and simmer for about 8 minutes until the pasta is *al dente*, which means 'firm to the bite' – *not* soggy! Drain and place in a bowl. ▶

350 g (12 oz) wholewheat
  macaroni
50 g (2 oz) butter
1 heaped tablespoon plain
  flour
750 ml (1¼ pint) milk
175 g (6 oz) cheese, grated
1 teaspoon English mustard
½ teaspoon salt
¼ teaspoon freshly ground
  black pepper
8 tomatoes, sliced
2 slices bread, made into
  breadcrumbs
2 teaspoons dried mixed
  herbs

1

STEP 2

In a saucepan, melt the butter. Add the flour and cook, stirring constantly with a whisk for 2 minutes, and then slowly add the milk and continue to stir until the mixture starts to thicken and looks like custard. (Don't worry if it takes a while to thicken!)

STEP 4

Mix the pasta with the sauce. Pour half the pasta and sauce into an ovenproof dish, cover with half the sliced tomatoes, and then pour over the other half.

' If you pour a tiny amount of oil in with the pasta when it's boiling, it helps to stop it sticking. '

STEP 3

⚡ Stir in 100g (4 oz) of the cheese, the mustard and salt and pepper, and continue to stir until smooth. Take off the heat.

STEP 5

Top with the remaining sliced tomatoes, the breadcrumbs, remaining grated cheese and the herbs.

⚡ Bake in the oven for 20 to 25 minutes until golden on top. Serve with a green salad.

'**Don't overcook pasta – there's nothing worse than soggy pasta!**'

CARROT AND COURGETTE CAKE

I know this sounds like a strange combination, but trust me – this tastes out of this world, is no problem to make at all, and no one will *ever* believe it contains vegetables!

STEP **1**

✦ Pre-heat the oven to gas mark 4, 180°C (350°F). Grease a 23 cm (9 in) cake tin. In a large bowl, mix the eggs, sugar, soured cream, carrots and courgettes really well. Then, whilst stirring, slowly pour in the oil until it is mixed together thoroughly. ▶

MAKES 1 × 23CM (9 IN) CAKE

2 eggs
175 g (6 oz) brown sugar
75 g (3 oz) soured cream
100 g (4 oz) carrots, peeled and grated
50 g (2 oz) courgettes, peeled and grated
85 ml (3 fl oz) sunflower oil
225 g (8 oz) self-raising wholemeal flour
¼ teaspoon baking powder
1 teaspoon mixed spice
50 g (2 oz) raisins

1

STEP **2**

In another bowl, mix together the flour, baking powder, spice and raisins. Then add this to the other mixture and blend until a lump-free batter is formed.

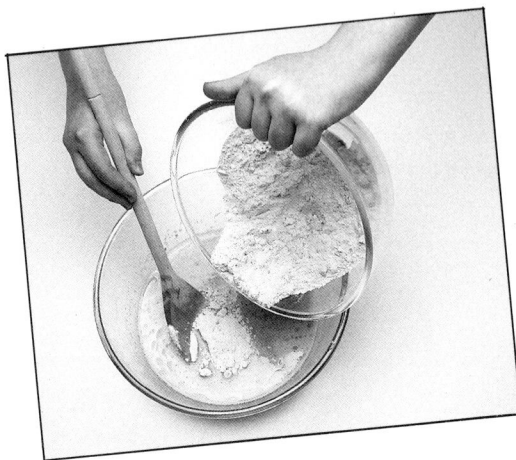

STEP **4**

Leave in the tin to cool for 5 minutes, then turn out on to a wire cooling rack. Before slicing into squares, you might like to add a touch of cream cheese icing and decorate with some grated orange and lemon rind . . .

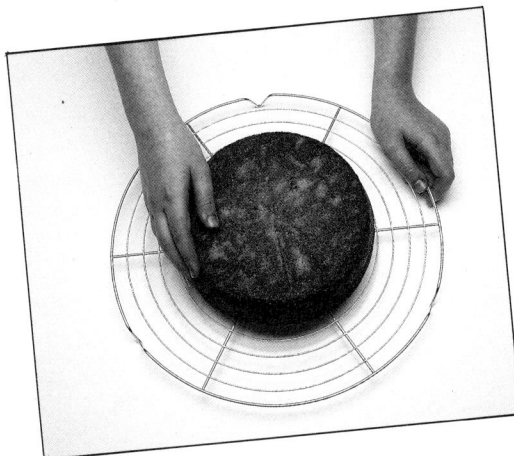

CREAM CHEESE ICING

175 g (6 oz) cream cheese
175 g (6 oz) icing sugar
½ teaspoon vanilla essence
Juice of ¼ lemon or 1
    tablespoon orange juice

Mix everything together until well combined.

3

⚡ Pour into the cake tin and bake in the oven for 25 to 30 minutes, or until a knife comes out clean and the top is risen and golden.

' *This actually tastes great as it is – really moist and gooey – but if you want it to be more sinful, try spreading it with Cream Cheese Icing (see below), topped with some grated orange and lemon rind.* '

BRILLIANT BREAD

You can't fail with this bread recipe, and once you've made your own, you may never want to buy bread again! If you experiment with different shapes and added ingredients, an exotic bread can also make a great gift!

STEP 1 Put the flours, yeast and salt in a mixing bowl. Add the margarine and rub with your fingertips until it resembles fine breadcrumbs (or use a mixer).

STEP 2 Add the honey, then the warm water and slowly mix it into the flour until it combines and forms a ball. You might need to add a couple of extra handfuls of flour if it looks too sticky. ▶

225 g (8 oz) strong
   wholemeal flour
225 g (8 oz) strong plain
   flour
25 g (1 oz), fast-action dried
   yeast (1 sachet)
1½ teaspoons salt
40 g (1½ oz) margarine, cut
   into pieces
1 teaspoon honey
300 ml (10 fl oz) warm
   water
1 egg, beaten

1

2

STEP **3** Place the dough on a well floured surface and knead for about 5 minutes, adding extra flour to stop it sticking, until the dough becomes smooth and elastic. Then place it back in the mixing bowl, cover with a tea towel and leave in a warm place for about 30 minutes, until the dough has risen and doubled in size.

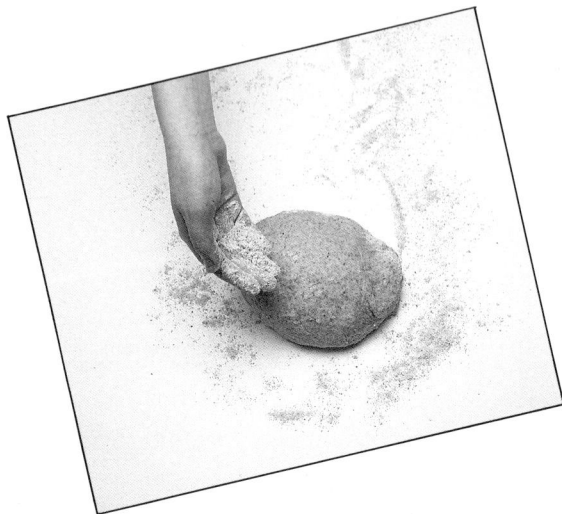

For a warming snack, why not try a big bowl of soup served with a hunk of your home-made bread . . .

S U P E R   S O U P

SERVES 4

50 g (2 oz) butter
½ small onion, peeled and
    chopped
1 cup any chopped vegetables
2 potatoes, peeled and
    chopped
2 chicken or vegetable stock
    cubes
600 ml (1 pint) water
1 handful long-grain rice
1 tablespoon tomato purée
Salt and freshly ground black
    pepper

Melt the butter in a saucepan, add the onion and cook until transparent. Add the rest of the vegetables and stir for a couple of minutes. Dissolve the stock cubes in the boiling water and pour this over the vegetables. Add the rice, tomato purée and salt and pepper to taste, and simmer gently over a low heat for about 15 minutes until all the vegetables are cooked.

4

⚡ Pre-heat the oven to gas mark 4, 180°C (350°F). Grease a baking sheet.

When the dough has risen, make it into shapes. Cut the dough with a blunt knife and mould it into whatever shapes you like . . . plaits, twists, rolls, loaves, gophers! Then place on the baking sheet, brush with a little egg, and bake in the oven for 25 to 30 minutes. The length of time will depend on the different shapes. Check the bread after 20 minutes and take it out when it sounds hollow when tapped on the bottom and it is risen and brown. Place on a wire rack to cool.

' Why not try spicing this recipe up to make different types of bread. Add 50 g (2 oz) of grated cheese, or 25 g (1 oz) of poppy seeds, or 50 g (2 oz) of raisins mixed with 25 g (1 oz) of chopped walnuts, or 50 g (2 oz) of chopped onion and 2 tablespoons of any dried herbs. Remember to add the extra ingredients <u>after</u> the dough has been left to rise. '

POTATO SKIN CRISPS

These are a much healthier alternative to your normal crisp, and they are also far more unusual – but, better than that, they taste wonderful. Eat them as they are or with a dip.

STEP 1

⚡ Pre-heat the oven to gas mark 6, 200°C (400°F). Wash and scrub the potatoes, and pierce several holes in their skins. Then with some kitchen paper, rub the skins with a little sunflower oil before putting them in the hot oven. It will depend on the size of each potato as to how long they will take to cook, but it should be anywhere between 45 and 60 minutes. You can tell if they're done by putting on an oven glove and giving them a squeeze. If they're squidgy, they're done!

STEP 2

Leave the potatoes to cool for 10 to 15 minutes, then slice them in half and scoop out the middle. Don't throw the potato away, save it for something else! Slice each potato skin half in two and lay them in well-greased muffin tins so that they have a curved shape. ▶

1 baking potato (per person)
Sunflower oil
Salt and freshly ground
 black pepper
Parmesan cheese, grated
 (optional)
Herbs (optional)

1

2

STEP **3**

⚡ Brush each one on both sides with some more oil, sprinkle with a little salt and pepper, and then put under the grill for about 5 minutes. When they are done you may like to sprinkle them with Parmesan cheese and chopped herbs and serve with a dip of your choice.

There are millions of different dips but here are two of my favourites . . .

TUNA FISH PATE

2 × 185 g (6½ oz) tins tuna, drained
2 tablespoons creamed horseradish
50 g (2 oz) butter, melted
Freshly ground black pepper, to taste
200 g (7 oz) cream cheese
2 tablespoons natural yoghurt
Juice of 1 lemon
2 tablespoons mayonnaise

Mix everything together, either in a bowl using a fork, or in a food processor. Pour either into one large dish or into several small ones. Cover and leave in the fridge for at least 1 hour before serving. Serve with toast, crackers or raw vegetable sticks.

SPEEDY GUACAMOLE

2 ripe avocados, peeled and
   stoned
Juice of ½ lemon
1 tomato, skinned and finely
   chopped
1 tablespoon finely chopped
   spring onion or chives
2 tablespoons soured cream
2 tablespoons mayonnaise
Salt and freshly ground black
   pepper, to taste

Mix all the ingredients together
and serve with potato skin
crisps, toast, crackers or raw
vegetable sticks.

CHRISTMAS TREE COOKIES

These are great because not only are they decorative but they are edible too. You can make and eat them any time of the year, but they're best made at Christmas to hang on your tree, or to use as edible gift tags, as presents in a box, or just to have around.

STEP 1 Beat together the butter and sugar in a bowl until light and creamy. Then add the flour, salt and spices (or cocoa powder).

STEP 2 Add the egg yolk, cold water and vanilla essence, and mix until the mixture pulls together and forms a ball. Wrap the ball of dough in a piece of kitchen foil and chill in the fridge for 1 hour. ▶

MAKES ABOUT 24 COOKIES

100 g (4 oz) butter
100 g (4 oz) caster sugar
225 g (8 oz) plain flour
A large pinch of salt
½ teaspoon ground ginger
    and ½ teaspoon
    cinnamon or allspice, or 2
    heaped tablespoons
    cocoa powder plus an
    extra tablespoon of water
1 egg yolk
½ tablespoon cold water
½ teaspoon vanilla essence

1

2

STEP **3** Pre-heat the oven to gas mark 6, 200°C (400°F). Grease 2 baking sheets. Roll the chilled dough out on a well-floured surface to about 5 mm (1/4 in) thick and stamp or cut out as many shapes as you want.

STEP **4** Place the shapes on the baking sheets and make a hole to hang them with, using a skewer or cocktail stick.
✦ Bake in the oven for 10 to 15 minutes, or until golden.

STEP **5** Leave to cool and harden on a wire rack, then decorate with coloured icing – 225g (8 oz) icing sugar, 2 tablespoons of water plus any food colouring. Thread with string or ribbon.